Bryan Johnson
Sponsored this book

CREATURES IN WHITE

SNOWY OWLS

To Tom, my best friend.

With special thanks to Dr. Leonard Soucy, President of The Raptor Trust, for reading my manuscript and so generously sharing his vast knowledge of snowy owls with me. My thanks also to naturalist Mimi Glass for recounting her wonderful snowy owl experiences.

W.P.

Text copyright ©1997 by Wendy Pfeffer.

Published by Silver Press
A Division of Simon & Schuster
299 Jefferson Road, Parsippany, NJ 07054

Designed by Brooks Design

Printed in the United States of America

ISBN 0-382-39323-6 (LSB) 10 9 8 7 6 5 4 3 2 1
ISBN 0-382-39322-8 (PBK) 10 9 8 7 6 5 4 3 2 1

Library of Congress Cataloging-in-Publication Data

Pfeffer, Wendy
Snowy owls/by Wendy Pfeffer.
p. cm.–(Creatures in White)
Summary: Describes the life cycle of this creature of the Arctic region in the far north.
1. Snowy owl–Juvenile literature. [1. Snowy owl. 2. Owls] I. Title. II. Series: Pfeffer, Wendy. Creatures in White.
QL696.S83P44 1996 96-16961
598.9'7-dc 20 CIP AC

Photo credits: Photo research: Susan Van Etten; Cover, ©Henry Ausloos/Animals, Animals; title page: ©Mark Wilson/Wildshot; p. 4-5, ©Dr. E.R. Degginger; 6-7, ©Harry M. Walker/Alaska Stock Images; 8-9, ©John Warden/Alaska Stock Images; 10-11, ©N. A. Chapell/Animals, Animals; 12-13, ©T.R. Fitzharris/Masterfile; 14-15, ©Steven Kaufman/Peter Arnold, Inc.; 16-17, © Francois Gohier/Photo Researchers, Inc.; 18-19, ©Ronald Curtis/ Masterfile; 20-21, ©Karl & Steven Maslowski/Photo Researchers, Inc.; 22-23, ©Cordier/Photo Researchers, Inc.; 24-25, ©Karl & Steven Maslowski/Photo Researchers, Inc.; 26-27, ©Mike Marcri/Masterfile; 28-29, ©Jean F. Stoick/Peter Arnold, Inc.; 30, t, ©Richard Kolar/Animals, Animals; 30, b, ©Alan D. Carey/Photo Researchers, Inc.; 31, t, ©E.R. Degginger/Animals, Animals; 31, b, ©IFA/Peter Arnold, Inc.; end paper, ©Martin Rogers/ Stock Boston; back cover, ©Alan D. Carey/Photo Researchs, Inc.

CREATURES IN WHITE

SNOWY OWLS

by Wendy Pfeffer

Silver Press

Parsippany, New Jersey

Near the North Pole in a cold land called the Arctic, a male snowy owl perches on a mound of frozen earth. On this hummock, his white feathers blend with the drifting snow and almost camouflage him.

Dense white feathers on the snowy owl's body make his coat waterproof and windproof. Bristly white feathers around the owl's golden eyes form his "face mask." And thick white feathers on his legs and feet protect them like warm slipper socks.

In winter the snowy owl's world, a large, flat, tree-less plain called the tundra, stays dark . . . all day and all night. In spring the sun appears for the first time in five months and lights up the tundra. This white wilderness contains frozen rivers, frosted fields, and ice-covered meadows.

For hours the beautiful white bird sits alone on the summit of the hummock without moving. He grasps his perch with sharp claws, called talons. This white owl of the Arctic is hungry.

His keen ears listen for small, fat, furry, rodents called lemmings. Inside tunnels, under the snow, they nibble on grasses.

The great white bird of prey turns his head in the direction of a sound. He lifts his broad wings, takes off, and glides close to the ground.

Suddenly his wings fold in flight. He swoops down. With his powerful legs and long, curved talons, he plunges into the snow, grabs one of the lemmings, and carries it off to his perch.

Each spring the tundra becomes active. Arctic foxes yelp and yap to find mates. Above the foxes, ravens circle. Beneath the foxes, lemmings stay busy . . . raising litters of lemmings.

Grasses, bushes, and mosslike plants called lichens, appear. The lemmings poke their heads out of the snow to eat this low growing carpet of green.

In May the snowy-white owl spreads his wings to travel in search of a mate. His mating cry, "WUFFF-WUFFF-WUCK, WUFFF-WUFFF-WUCK," echoes over the vast tundra.

A female snowy owl hears the call and answers in a higher pitched voice, "WUFFF-WUFFF-WUCK, WUFFF-WUFFF-WUCK."

The male flies to the female's hummock. He bows, fluffs his feathers, and swaggers about, dipping his wingtips as he performs his courtship strut.

The pure white male and the female, with dark brown flecks on her feathers, look like patches of snow and brown earth. The male is whiter than the female, but she is bigger and weighs more. The mated pair stay together on the hummock.

The male leans forward. He puffs his throat, raises his tail, and calls out, "WHOOOO . . . WHOOOO . . . WHOOOO . . . WHOOOO." His deep-pitched call tells other owls that this is his territory.

Around the middle of June, the female scratches the top of their hummock. She scoops some earth from the center, then swirls herself around until she's comfortable in the shallow hole.

When the female lays the first egg in the nest, she sits on it right away. During the next fifteen days, she lays four more pure white eggs. While the female sits on the eggs, the male hunts for mice, lemmings, grouse, and hares.

A grouse wanders by. The snowy owl takes off. He captures the grouse and carries it back to his mate.

After the pair enjoy their feast, the female places feathers around the rim of the nest to keep her clutch of eggs warm. The male flies to another hummock, not far from the nest.

In this treeless land, hummocks make perfect lookout posts. The male watches the grass for lemmings. He scans the rocky ground for enemies. And he stands guard, defending his family, as a hungry arctic fox slinks past the nest to steal eggs.

The snowy owl stands tall on both feet, puffing up his feathers. He makes a clicking sound, spreads his wings, and glares at the fox with his large yellow eyes.

But the owl doesn't scare the hungry fox. Quickly, the owl leaves his hummock. His powerful wings make a long downstroke and a fast upstroke. The flight is swift and short. He lands beside the female, leans back, and defends with both feet.

Using his powerful legs the owl spikes the fox with his long, sharp talons. The injured fox flees and the owl returns to his hummock. His family is safe.

After thirty-two days, the first egg that was laid, hatches. The chick stays with the four unhatched eggs under their mother. On her belly a "brood patch" has formed where feathers have shed. The chick snuggles up to this warm spot and waits for its father to bring food.

Every few days another chick hatches. The oldest owlet, already covered with thick down, acts like a blanket for the younger chicks and unhatched eggs.

When the oldest owlet is about nine days old, long, thick, fluffy, gray down gradually replaces the white down. The owlet looks as if it's covered with soot instead of snow.

Thirty-two days after the last egg was laid, the last owlet hatches. The oldest owlet is nearly two weeks old. The five nestlings snuggle under their mother's warm brood patch. They nibble at their mother's bill and feathers to tell her they want food . . . mice, birds, and lemmings.

After the last chick hatches, the mother owl still broods her young chicks to keep them warm. The father still hunts. As they grow, the chicks demand so much food that the mother has to leave the nest to hunt, too. The owlets make soup-slurping noises to tell they're hungry. The oldest owlet opens its mouth wide. . . wide enough to swallow a whole mouse.

When a chick is about sixteen days old, it leaves the nest. The chicks scatter close to the hummock. When the soot-colored chicks gather together and sit perfectly still, they look like a pile of rocks.

In summer the Arctic tundra stays light . . . all day and all night. Ice melts. Flowers sprout. Insects swarm. Millions of birds migrate north to the snowy owl's world. More birds mean more food for the owls.

The young snowy owls eat and grow and change. White feathers appear around their eyes. Gradually thick white feathers hide most of the soft, sooty–gray down.

By seven weeks the young owls are feathered for the cold winter ahead. They jump and flap their wings, getting ready to fly. By eight weeks the fledglings can fly. In late summer the millions of birds who migrated north, begin their migration south.

Some fledgling owls may fly south, too, where there's more food. Their parents sometimes migrate. But, there are enough lemmings to eat this year so the older snowies stay in the Arctic for the cold winter.

Spring finally arrives with lichens for the lemmings to eat, and lemmings for the owls to eat. The owls' mating cry, "WUFFF-WUFFF-WUCK, WUFFF-WUFFF-WUCK" echoes over the tundra again.

And soon the great white hunters of the Arctic produce another family of white snowy owls.

Owl Facts

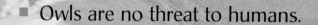

- Owls are no threat to humans.

- Owls are raptors, or predators. They capture animals with their talons, so they have food to survive.

- Since snowy owl chicks grow so quickly they need lots of food. Each one pound chick can eat three or four lemmings a day. This is equal to a fifty pound child eating two hundred hamburger patties a day.

- Six week old snowy owls stand about one foot tall with a wingspan of up to three feet. Adult snowies are about two feet tall, with a wingspan of about five feet.

- It is illegal in the United States and Canada to kill or harm an owl. It is also illegal to possess an owl, living or dead, or any parts of an owl, even a feather, without a permit.

- Snowy owls usually mate for life.

- The hearing of most owls is so extraordinary that they can locate and capture prey they can't even see.

- An owl turns its head to see sideways, since it can't move its eyes. All owls have twice as many neck bones as humans do. Therefore, any owl can turn its head much further around than people can.

- Most owls are nocturnal, which means they are active at night. Snowy owls are also diurnal, which means active during the day, because the Arctic summer is light, all day and all night.

- Snowy owls can live for nearly thirty five years in captivity. In the wild, snowy owls may live seventeen years.

WHERE IN THE WORLD
ARE SNOWY OWLS ?

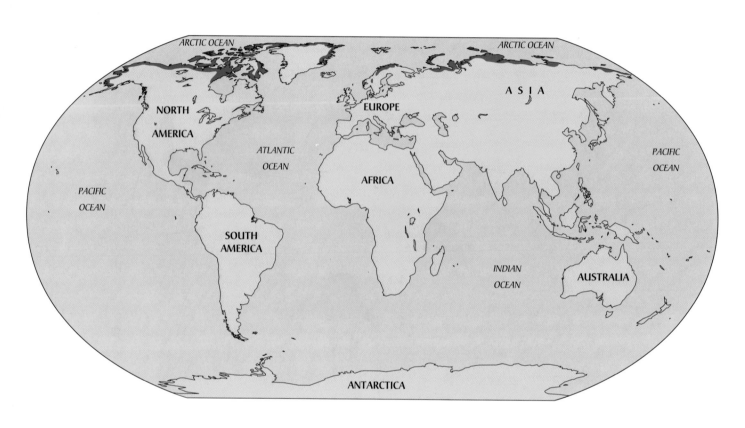

■ Snowy Owls live here